# In Between

# In Between

## Sumedha Jena

BLACK EAGLE BOOKS
2021

BLACK EAGLE BOOKS

USA address:
7464 Wisdom Lane
Dublin, OH 43016

India address:
E/312, Trident Galaxy, Kalinga Nagar,
Bhubaneswar-751003, Odisha, India

E-mail: info@blackeaglebooks.org
Website: www.blackeaglebooks.org

First International Edition Published by
BLACK EAGLE BOOKS, 2021

**IN BETWEEN**
by **Sumedha Jena**

Copyright © **Sumedha Jena**

All rights reserved. No part of this publication may be reproduced, stored in a retrieval system, or transmitted, in any form or by any means, electronic, mechanical, photocopying, recording or otherwise without the prior permission of the publisher.

Cover & Interior Design: Ezy's Publication

ISBN- 978-1-64560-214-9 (Paperback)
Library of Congress Control Number: 2021947118

Printed in United States of America

# Dedicated To

My Grandfather (Jeje)
Professor Bairagi Charan Jena

# Review Notes

When one reads poems written by a young person, one ordinarily expects them to express the joys and sorrows of growing up, and hopes and aspirations animating a young mind dreaming of and dreading the future. One also expects to share the anxieties oppressing the heart of someone who has not had the benefit of age and experience. However, a pleasant surprise awaited me when I started going through poems written by Sumedha put together in this collection. They reveal a whole new world of possibilities and a sensibility shaped by sober reflections on life and its many ironies. They are infused with a quiet intensity and convey a melancholy awareness of a world facing an unanticipated calamity. No wonder, the young poet feels the 'weight of the world ' on her shoulders. The reader quickly moves away from the external world encompassing the poet towards an interior landscape presented evocatively but without sentimentality or self-indulgence. During this journey, questions arising in her mind lead her to explore impenetrable mysteries of life to which easy answers can never be found. Who can, for instance, answer the question, 'Does the light stop where the dark begins?' or 'Does the light cast its own shadow?'. But the questions and a restless search for answers to them lend the poem depth, complexity and a resonant beauty.

I am confident that, as she grows older and finds new ways of experiencing and interpreting the world, Sumedha will find a distinctive voice which will render her poems more memorable and more richly meaningful.

**Jatindra Kumar Nayak**
Former Professor of English,
Utkal University, Odisha
Professor Emeritus,
KISS Deemed to be University, Odisha

# Preface

Poetry has had an influential impact on my life for the longest period of time. Writing in general has always come easy to me, while I struggled with practically anything else. However, writing this book wasn't the smoothest journey. After I had written and published my last book in April of 2020, I struggled with writer's block. For several months, I had tried to use any external influence to help me write, but at the end of the day, I had come up with nothing. Majority of this reason was due to the global pandemic in which everyone remained trapped inside their houses for months. I barely stepped outside to even see the sun, and remained in one corner of my house. Due to this, no creative guidance was able to help me get words down my page.

After suffering from writer's block for a while, I got a sudden rush of hypergraphia; in which it pushed me to write my first poem. While I would jot down any random thought into my notes and then have it written, this wasn't the end to all the difficulties that I had to face. Throughout the process of writing this book, I was in my junior year of high school. It is a well known fact that, that year is one of the hardest years of your high school career. It was not easy trying to manage the stress I induced from school and while also trying to write any emotional thoughts I endured in the meanwhile. Mentally, I was completely done and it felt like I was at my breaking point. I knew I wanted to keep writing enough to be able to create a book, so I could bring a sanguine energy while the world suffers silently during the pandemic. And I also wanted to keep balancing my schoolwork on top of it, which was not an easy task to tackle. While I could have finished and published the book early this year, I had to take countless breaks which just delayed the publication.

Once the school year gradually began to ease its workload, I eventually began to finish up any unfinished poems or revise any that I didn't think were good enough. I spent the majority of my summer going back in and just kept re-editing on my own until I thought they were ready to go into the official editing process. One would assume that the journey that one undergoes in writing poetry would be simple, because how difficult could it possibly be to write down how you feel? It goes to show that any path that you choose to take won't necessarily be a simple one, however it's how you choose to come out of it that truly determines who you are as a person.

Throughout the process of writing this book, I have had several sources of motivation and inspiration. I decided to not stick with a singular theme with this book or have it revolve around abstract ideas. The topics of my poems had a variation. Some would center about nature and focus on it's beauty. While others would cover a conceptual feeling. All in all, I decided to not have this book zero in on an actual theme. It is why I had decided to name the book, "In Between," because even though it is vague it contains vivid details of a specific topic if you look into it hard enough.

While on the topic of inspiration, I took a lot of my creativity from William Wordsworth. William Wordsworth was an English poet who had helped fuel the Romantic Age in English literature. Essentially, he is known to be one of the founders of the Romanticism era in English literature. He is known to be a "Poet of nature," even calling himself "A Worshipper of Nature." His poems about the world of nature were so filled with vivid imagery that one would feel like you are in the place he is writing about. He was also well known for his lyrical ballads which just enhanced the beauty of his poems.

Even though I didn't necessarily write my poems in his exact style, his poems about nature are what inspired me to write about the wonderfulness of the world outside. While being stuck inside our houses for months and not being able to enjoy the world of nature, I wanted to simply bring extra attention to what we have missed seeing, and help people realize the importance of the environment we are surrounded with.

Another influence whose path I had followed was Edgar Allan Poe. He is known for his mysterious and cryptic poetry and short stories, and majority of them have overlapping themes as well. He included elements such as dark romanticism and primarily focused on themes that included regret, love, and horror. What inspired me about Poe is how he would take something so dark and mysterious and be able to capture the imaginative minds of many readers, by turning them into something so beautiful.

I too, had explored certain "dark" themes or what would be considered dark at my age. I did this to establish the fact that poetry doesn't necessarily have to carry a light, upbringing, and positive meaning. It could sometimes contain its' complete opposite. Edgar Allan Poe told stories in an imaginative and creative way, and while again, I didn't do the exact same thing, I tried to incorporate certain elements from his poems into mine.

These two poets have been a longtime favorite of mine, and I tried to use their work as best as I could because of how inspired I felt by them in the moment. In my previous book, I had just written down any emotion I had felt, however I tried to integrate certain components from both Wordsworth and Poe as I believe they are great poets who have done such wonderful work throughout their lifetime. They both carry contrasting themes to each other, which led me to take their opposing styles and place it into one book.

All things considered, this book was a blessing to write even though I faced some difficulties in the process. I would like to take a moment to thank everyone who had pushed me to complete this, even when I felt like I couldn't. I didn't think any form of motivation would be able to help me until I received it from my own family and friends. It is because of them I was able to finish what I had started.

I would like to thank Dr. Jatindra Kumar Nayak who assisted me in reviewing and making the book the best version of itself. I appreciate his time and effort into analyzing what I have written and leaving any feedback; giving room for me to improve.

■■

# CONTENTS

| | |
|---:|---:|
| Chaos | 15 |
| Reflection | 17 |
| Wake up | 19 |
| 6ft Underwater | 21 |
| My mirror self | 23 |
| Nature's tears | 25 |
| Red | 26 |
| A personal vacation | 28 |
| Feeling a little green | 30 |
| Blow out your candles | 32 |
| A language unspoken | 34 |
| Eyes closed | 36 |
| 143 | 37 |
| Abendrot | 39 |
| Heavy eyes | 40 |
| Ripple | 42 |
| In between | 44 |
| Lonely | 45 |
| One in a million | 47 |
| 6 Feet apart | 49 |
| Inside out | 51 |
| Heart and head | 53 |
| 7 deadly sins | 55 |
| Your eyes | 57 |
| A last choice | 59 |
| 4 Elements (haiku) | 61 |
| Insomnia | 62 |
| Growth | 64 |
| Pollution | 65 |
| Present. not future | 67 |
| Dead ends | 69 |

# Chaos

a surge of fear deluges the crowd
screams of panic overfill the streets
I cannot see anything behind
the tears that well in my eyes

a sick plague takes over the globe
taking us out one by one
separated from our families
we all slowly succumb to the disease

the world collapses into a solemn silence
pushing everyone to the edge of their seats
trapped inside while we watch the world
while this dismay empowers us

with each day; down to the minute
numbers keep increasing
lives fall dramatically
when is this ever going to end?

we thought it couldn't get worse
but all proceeded in a downward spiral
they call it the first wave
the onset of our collapse

they say survival is brave
through the obscurity of this time
vacant roads, full of old conversations
how long can we stay away?

unable to be in their presence
so we give in to the solitude
and the grays turn into blues
the air starts to cleanse

creatures of the day parade the roads
the purge seemingly meets its end
our celestial sphere begins to open up
beginning its slow healing process

everything is alright in the world again, right? No.
ignorance in humans comes to a head
incapable in staying away
the second wave eradicates millions
we come back to square one

a constant cycle of death
and it will never be at a finish
continuous decline
a chaos we brought ourselves into

# Reflection

I come home from outside
running while the wind passes by
a cheerful aura glistens above me
an angelic light guiding my way


flashbacks of my youth begin to play
a memory of my inner childishness
so much time has passed since
it all seems light years away


I wish to go back to those days
where I carried not a single care for the world
I lived according to my own terms
a happier era


I walk into my bathroom
and I stare into the depressingly ornate mirror
I bend down to wash my face
and I look up to see someone unrecognizable

a grown up woman in front of me
all the happiness stripped away
my smile fades completely
my eyes crinkle softly


as I gaze at the place
where that little girl used to be

# Wake up

every single night
a different horror replaying
an efflux of fear keeps me up
I can't stop shaking


a constant nightmare
playing like a record
makes me fearful of going to sleep
what if they reach out to me


what if they pull me into an obscurity
where I am just alone for them to haunt
every unfinished thought
just sitting there awaiting


poking fun at my misery
another form of haunted evil
sending cold shivers down my spine
finding its claws into my mind

a prisoner trapped in a perpetual loop
flashes of a mysterious apparition
drawing me in too close
but at what cost?


a string of forbidden errors
void of sound sleep
a blank existence I'm living in
becoming a race to keep me up

## 6ft Underwater

feeling entirely senseless
leaving troublesome energies behind
as I dive underneath
to re-cleanse my soul

holding my wavering breath
swimming in the open
a leverage that my body carries over me
slowly draining out my single life force

my body steadily tightens
with each slow-passing second
getting in touch with myself again
sensing every pain and emotion

and I fall in more deeply
while the oxygen in me fades
but I regain control
fighting for the surface

the air struggles to reach my lungs
my shoulder relax as I reach up
heading out from the deep-end
but a strong desire pulls me back

wanting to deluge myself again
to get a moment of freedom
feels like a drug waiting to overtake me
ready to just overdose

fighting back while my body refuses
keeping steady while I go under
a wave of calm swims over me.
swimming towards the bright light overhead

I reach towards a steady hand reaching out
an angelic voice calling for me.
coming back up from the azure lined depths
the ones that were 6ft underwater.

# My mirror self

an instant ignited fire
I see what I see in myself in you
and it drives me crazy
all my bad morphed into a single person
everything I hate about myself
just reflecting like a mirror back at me

I look at you and I feel like home
a unique and zealous bond that we share
becoming the ying to my yang
a cloud of endless toxicity.
together we are just unstoppable

like two souls connected from different universes
just the two of us in our own little world
we were doomed from the beginning
rotating between enemies to soul mates
always clashing right into each other

you always knew exactly what I needed
knew me before I even knew myself
a magnetic feeling just drawing me close
but pushing me away at the same time

constantly chasing each other
a cycle that I never seem to get tired of
an honest and unconditional bond that we can't have
since neither of us can love ourselves first

an unfamiliar dynamic but so unique
dwelling right into the unknown
you push me to be the better version of myself
but sometimes that is unattainable

something had exploded in the universe
the day I encountered you
shaken by the intensity of the bond we feel
and I try taking my time to understand you

while we both wish the blissful feeling to last forever
because we want that euphoric connection to stay
the catastrophe that awaits hits harder
leading to a downward spiral of betrayal

how I wished you were perfect
but you are just a mirror of me
while you keep chasing me
I feel the rush from running away

What we share never ends well
alas I wait.
for our paths to cross each other's again
maybe this time it would be the one to last.

# Nature's tears

the smell of the fresh path of grass
lies beneath my feet
I lie down and gaze up at the chalky sky
awaiting for nature's tears to fall and caress my face

it opens its exposed self to me
welcoming me with open arms
a musical beat plays as each drop hits the ground
and I let my umbrella fly away

truly the greatest season of the year
as it arrives to wash away the heat
the humid breeze brushes over the paved land
while I look at awe at the beauty above me

sweet, sweet rain bestowing upon me

# Red

like the sound of a blaring alarm
telling everyone to get up in the morning
waking up every nerve in my body
feels like I'm on fire

fire comes our way with its blazing flames
the smells of burning fumes inhaled
a poisonous toxin electrifying me
painful charred burns come take its place

the blaring danger it poses as
and we see it in our daily lives
stopping us in the paths we choose to take
but something keeps pushing me forward

a touch of freedom
just kept at the edge of my fingertips
keeps me unhinged for a familiar feeling
for just a blast of simple adventure

a memorabilia of falling in love
the initial sweetness takes you by surprise
connecting with another like a missing piece
someone to share your spirit and soul

eyes glowing a luminescent shade
uncontrollable shaking just takes over
can't even fathom the pain I feel right now
I can hear my heartbeat through my body

being a portrayal of my passion
the many aspects of my life I fight for
my very ambition representing me as a person
shown by a singular color

# A personal vacation

freshly brewed coffee sitting next to me
I tap my foot lightly to a mellow rhythm
my nail bitten fingers fiddle with the hem of my shirt
a somber silence fills the air around me

I anticipate whether I should pick up this book
whether this one would lead to a burrow of adventure
whether I would be entering a new world
a safe place that I could hole up in

I stare in excitement at the cover
as it burns a hole in the back of my head
I eye the yellowed pages from its years in a dusty corner
and the worn out spine, in danger of falling apart

as I flip onto the first page each word burns bright
the letters fly off the page and into my mind
creating a whirlwind of carefully structured sentences
that heaves me away to another land

one minute I'm falling down into a tunnel
and the other I'm placing my foot into a glass slipper
then I'm flying away to a faraway land

each chapter fulfills a different aspiration
checking off a fantastical mental bucket list
seems like I'm travelling all over the place
with my feet still stuck to the ground

an intense wrapping of emotions
that seems to consume me whole with each line
I want to hide myself inside the cover
and let each sentence tell its story

I don't think i ever want to leave this world
can't distinguish the line between reality and fantasy
I pick myself up from my book
and reflect on the marvelous journey I took

I place it back in its dusty shelf
as it waits for someone to partake in its endeavors'
I scour my eyes over the million possibilities
of which place I would like to go to next

## Feeling a little green

such a toxic feeling
as it rots me from inside out
deep-rooted in me as I watch myself seethe
over the people around me leaving

I feel the weight of the world on my shoulders
as I'm envious of the things that aren't mine
I question why I don't have what everyone else has
why can't I be like everyone else?

I'm possessive of the things I own
don't mind me when I don't share
unaware of whom I can really trust around me
my internal issues gradually build up

self sabotage my own relationships
because how I feel is beyond my control
maybe I'll end up getting replaced
I don't want my biggest fear coming true

a sudden loss of control
a concept I am not familiar with
don't try to convince me I'm irrational
I swear I just want what's best for us

why does he get more love and attention?
I ask myself what I did wrong now
I promise you that I will try harder
maybe you will look at me, the same way you look at him

it's hard to feel good about myself
everyone is so perfect and then there's me
I want to rid myself of this gut wrenching emotion
letting me know on how I am not good enough

and now I lie in my bed feeling dejected
why do I make myself feel this way?
no one understands what runs through my head
I really want to be better, I do.

# Blow out your candles

no one ever asks to be brought into the light
but we end up coming anyways
with a splash of splotchy red
and we take in our first breath


the day is to be celebrated for years to come
a day filled with momentous joy lies ahead
an invisible blanket of love wraps us comfortingly
and we don't even know what's happening


every single year, another party waits
little children having hundreds of people come
while some get lucky to even have five appear
different kinds of celebrations across the globe


why do we celebrate getting a year older?
in reality we just inch closer to our death
a cynical mentality that some carry
assuming someone isn't excited about growing up

the craving for a little sweetness calls for cake
as we place our candles and blow them to make a wish
they tell us our wishes will come true
keeping our small heart young forever


I realize that I'm just one step closer to the finish line
I relish the path that I am about to take
and I get ready for the years of hard work waiting
so I blow out my candles to make a wish

# A language unspoken

a sort of language where I don't even have to say a word
yet you will discover my entire life story
as it ranges from slow and mindless to quick and obscene
aesthetically pleasing to the eyes and the mind


I twirl my body to the sound of the music
as this becomes a moment of self expression
allows me to escape my soulful body
and dance beyond the barriers given to me


I begin to learn more about myself
why I am attracted to this form of art
and I let myself connect better with others around me
learning who they are with the swift movement of my feet


I showcase the raw emotions surging through my veins
a touch of euphoria glistens on my skin
set to resolve the troubles I face
providing an outlet for energy

developing an unspoken emotional connection
with the person whose hand I take
as we sway our bodies
to the rhythmic beauty


manifesting my inner passions
while being in a more stimulating environment
unable to simply stay in one place anymore
keeping me constantly on my toes


contributes in keeping me invigorated
achieving this feeling of contentment
appeals to every aspect of my soul
supplying me with a feeling of unity

# Eyes closed

vulnerability is a dangerous feeling
a hundred pair of eyes could be watching me
and I would never notice
as I place my hands over my eyes
limiting my sight as I see a void of color
a void of color which always leads to black
an occasional pop of color would steal the show
my vision feels much like a kaleidoscope
I can't see where I am going
however I sense where everything is
the feeling of shadowy people near starts to creep into me
like a big wall of black marked by lighter silhouette
I'm terrified of this unknown sensation
not knowing where I am about to go
my other existing senses get sharper
it's like walking in an endless maze
not knowing which turn to take to your way out
I want to be able to feel safe
safe and comforted
but I can't stand not knowing
not being able to detect what might happen next
as I take my hands off my eyes
to take in what I have been missing
the countless of colors filling in my brain
so I paint in the missing spaces to hide the gray

# 143

one of the world's most illustrious feelings
a fervor containing an unfulfilled passion ignited
a collection of everything you have ever felt
and then you finally meet someone
who's able to give you everything you ever needed

they come to you at your moment of weakness
at an unexpected time when you didn't think
you needed them
and you get swept off your feet
by someone who is shrouded with a golden aura
closing up that intrinsic void you carry heavily

promising the other to maintain this
unconditional feeling
and then they give you hope
a scary word to some who have been betrayed
but it's something you feel with your beating heart
and you receive the happiness of a lifetime

constantly carried the lowest expectations out of life
but now you are able to experience an intense set of emotions
as you finally hold yourself to an empathetic regard,
for someone who deserves you
they truly fit you like no other

a missing puzzle piece that seemed lost
had found its way to you to connect
an addictive rush that you savor each time
giving each other that final sense of contentment
a feeling you have wanted forever, you've finally gotten

every bone in your body craves for their presence
whilst you keep each other a special place in your hearts
they become your stable ground
in your moments of destruction
a strong hold they are able to have on you

a hundreds of faces in one room
however their set of eyes seem to only align with yours
a gush of fluttery feelings blanket your body
like fate that was written in the stars above
as they look at you like you're the only one in the room

and you deserve to fall for someone who just wants you.

# Abendrot

the sky is on fire.
a majestic scenery that is painted across worlds
with the touch of the sun's brush
as an invariant equatorial stretches beyond the horizon

where the red meets the orange
And the orange meets the yellow
as all the tempestuous colors come together
and unite to create a unique imagery

a desolate land overshadowed by a beauteous night sky
and I mourn for its limited time
cooling the world's children with its delightful umbrella
I gaze up to see the blooming of wild flowers

it's a picture that would last in your mind
for a thousand lifetimes and over
the rays from the yellow orb waves its goodbye
as it slowly sinks down into the earth

I want to dip my finger into the sky
and stir all the colors together
making the sky turn an everlasting pink
the sun leaves a mellow kiss for the world

the calm slowly arrives after

# Heavy eyes

the need to rest my eyes transcends my mind
my body lies weak as the bed stands underneath
a hypnotic wave that makes me drop dead
spots of gray appear before my eyes


my brain feels like falling out of my head
it's too heavy I can't move myself
no quick movement comes out of me
the strenuous pressure from my brain makes me ache


I sense my consciousness pulling away from me
I needed to give in to the narcotic feeling
no longer being able to keep myself awake
never have I ever felt so weak to the power that clung to me


It seemed like an eternity ago when I felt like this
my vision kept blacking out
I had no recollection of what was taking place
I slowly start to drift off into a deep slumber

I longed for a serene night like this
a day I would be able to peacefully rest on my own
a moment filled with tranquility
a safe haven that welcomed me with open arms


the aching in my body ceases to exist
my heartbeat matches my slow breaths
a heavy veil seems to set on my eyes
I lay lifeless but alive in my abode


I greet the land of dreams as I begin to wander
as my conscious now flies free without restraints
as I rest still in my warm duvet covers
everything in sight becomes a pitch black

# Ripple

the water is a vigorous but majestic force
it has the power to give and also take away life
something as simple as a pebble can disrupt
the placidity of the water


so precious that I don't want to touch it
however its intense depth calls my name
I gently tap the surface of the water
and observe the eerie stillness of what I just touched


the subtle waves slowly move away from the center
it's as if they are united so they move at the same time
such an innocently beautiful moment


I wander around until I stumble across a smooth faced pebble
I look off into the distance and clutch the rock in my palm
as I channel my inner athlete to throw it across the stream
but it did not sink like I assumed it would

it skipped across the shallow water joyfully
until it plunged straight into the stream
each skip leaving a trail of seamless ripples
varying from all different kinds of sizes


miniscule waves that seem to turn into bigger waves
adding the rough texture to the serenity of the water
and the golden fish swim through the calm waves
leaving behind beautiful ripples

■

# In between

an opaque reminiscence
that lies in between
a place where light does not reach
and enter the other side
an absence of the white
gets masked by an ominous black
an undefined partition
that divides the two sides
but does the light stop where the dark begins?
a questionable mystery that lies within
does the light cast its own shadow?
or is it just a blurred enigma
it defines the surrounding world
and it blocks the path of the light
allowing for its shadowy friend to appear
a harmonious alliance one might perceive
the beaming light will shine through
but behind the light stands the darkness
and the gray just solemnly remains still
as a symbol of their bond
that continues for forever
remaining as an unanswerable question
as to what lies between the light and shadow

# Lonely

when you walk on an abandoned road
who remains next to you?
you turn your head to each side
but only see the shadow that follows behind

when you receive good news
who do you call when you pick up the phone?
you scroll through countless numbers
not a single one coming to view

a universal human feeling
yet you seem to be the only one feeling this way
and the idea plays its way into your state of mind
you are not alone yet feel isolated

surrounded by hundreds
but you can't even bring yourself to speak
given no sense of direction
a lack of purpose leaving your life meaningless

break yourself out of this vicious cycle
heal the empty abyss taking place in your heart
you become hungry for the feeling of loneliness
and now you can't leave

a persistent affliction going on forever
you naturally disassociate in an inescapable situation
an empty feeling in your stomach begins to form
blowing you up internally beyond your capacity

it takes up a personality of its own
becoming another hidden side of you
the feelings of unfulfilled love take root
the need for a permanent attachment grows stronger

you want to be able to help yourself
an inexorable reality
you are void of your true emotions
behind there lays your inner resentment

overburdened by the pain that you carry
is it really worth locking yourself in
you desire the feeling of comfort and security
break out of your shell as it lies in front of you

# One in a million

a sunflower in a field full of dandelions
a gem in a mountain of rocks
an oddball so eccentric from everyone else
but so wonderfully distinctive from the rest of us


you never really know what to say
unable to merge to a single harmony
striking a chord with whomever you run into
your peculiarity starts to shine through


but you don't want to fake who you are
marching to the beat of your own rhythm
you are special than other conforming souls
you are the epitome of a myriad of colors


no one will even ever begin to understand you
a perfect imperfection that you represent
and you follow no one but yourself
you are the leader to the journey you choose to take

you don't emulate yourself to fit in
a school of fish yet you swim the opposite way
and you develop the resilience to reject the world
you are not right but you are not wrong either


a beguiling quality that you possess,
you walk backwards as the world moves forward
you never look behind to see who notices
because you are stuck in your own dream world

# 6 Feet apart

how does one even make new friends?
what do you say to strike up a conversation?
these questions ponder in my head
as I eye the girl sitting 6 feet down from me


I want to sound interesting enough to someone else
will she even like who I am
I scoot a little closer to her
closing the distance to 5 feet.


I can feel her looking at the side of my head
is this the part where I make intense eye contact?
I fidget with my fingers and let out a deep breath
and lessen the space to 4 feet.


The silence is truly deafening
as no one else chose to ride the subway today
I turn my head towards her and give her a smile
she reciprocates and moves closer. It is now 3 feet.

no one ever talks about how hard it is to talk to a stranger
you don't know a single thing about them
yet something pushes you to say hi
so I moved closer to make it 2 feet.


the first word that escaped my lips
was just a simple hello
and then it slowly unraveled
a million of conversation starters ran in my head


never did I think I would talk to an unfamiliar face
a sequence of laughter begin to fill the air
we both start to feel so warm and fuzzy
as we familiarize ourselves with each other. 1 foot.


and the trip comes to an end
where we have to part ways
but I had a conversation with a stranger
and that left me in a delightful mood all day

# Inside out

made up from a circle of emotions
and each one has a different grasp on us
but we place a mask on our face
to hide what we feel truly in the inside


one day we feel like an empty vessel
yet another we are filled with emotion
how does one even begin to understand others?
when they can't even understand themselves


it is like we are floating in space,
or just translucent clouds up in the sky,
who don't even know their own identity?
it is something we can no longer hide


do we even know how we feel in the inside?
so many questionable feelings
so many things to love and hate
but we are ambitious to figure ourselves out

we are just lonely souls roaming free
an adventurous spirit
as we grow on our own
like an obscure flower growing in a meadow


blessed to even enter into this world
we place ourselves around the things that give us happiness
we gaze upon the days that pass us by
as the question of who we are begins to fade

# Heart and head

an intimate bond that cycles through opposite directions
a relation to keep us alive
an influential source of life
controlling every decision we make


one speaks for how I feel
a subconscious voice telling me what to do
irrational choices that I tend to make
because I let my emotions override me


never wanting to be left in regret
an unstable, fluctuating thing, I choose to follow
clouding my judgment when faced with an obstacle
but it inspires me to do start something new


coaxing me into letting go of my expectations
and I know I'll run into my fears
developing a passion, that makes me want to persevere
acting as a driving force for the things I love

the other speaks for how I think
an advisor correcting my wrongs
and I fall into a deep paralysis
in an attempt to make the right choice


my indecisiveness should know better
I need to do everything the right way
however I'm left confused and on my own
a time where I require my calm rationality


dodging ever possibility to avoid my emotions
because that turns into a wreck
my spontaneous nature hides itself
so I approach every problem with caution


however the choice still lies with me
on whether I should trust my heart or my head
because one will ensure I am happier
while the other guarantees a steadier life

# 7 deadly sins

1.I like to assume I am better than everyone else
there is nothing I can possibly do wrong
graced by the Almighty above
believe in myself they all say
therefore I am the only one I listen to

2. why does everyone believe she is so beautiful?
what do I possibly lack that she possesses
I would curse her with a lifetime of odiousness
so she can finally understand what she deserves
because I need to be superior to her

3. I possess so much in my hands
but it is not enough. it is never enough
it seems to be like the hunger calls me
and I give in so easily so no one else can have it
I just want to have it all

4. I want to give myself up to everyone around me
the craving for someone to love grows increasingly
the strong desire for them to notice me is what I need
but I also pine for the finer things in life
a wanting to be pleasured all throughout

5. I can only ever feel true vexation in my veins
the idea of someone crossing me frustrates me to my core
no one in my opinion should be allowed to be happy
because nothing truly good exists in this world
therefore the only thing that runs in my mind is madness

6. they ask me why I am so affluent
because I take everything from everyone as it's all mine
no one deserves anything nice
it should all just belong to me
I get to keep it all to myself forever

7. what is the issue with me sleeping all day?
I want to avoid all forms of hard work
it is just not meant for me, I am telling you now
everyone else can do what they like
but if I don't have to, then I don't need to

# Your eyes

you ask me to describe a beautiful place
and that is what I proceed to do
I begin with telling you of scenery straight out of a painting
so magnificent that it would shock you senseless
the magenta colored petals lean forward
and I take one into my hand as I look at its veins
with all of them heading into different directions
like they each have a unique purpose in life
I let the branch prop back to its original position
I change my viewpoint to the off-distanced mountain
as it is covered by certain haziness
but you can still take notice of the distinctive trees
that clings to the mountainside
and it hides a wooden trail where you see tiny heads
just treading upwards in hopes to reach a destination
and just like the invigorating wind takes my focus away
behind each majestic tree lies a much longer one
it stands upright however it is plain and mossy
while one would notice the lilac tree in the front
I noticed the ordinary and unadorned sapling
standing behind
nature is truly a wonder on our planet
I then gaze upon what's front of me and i see a mirror
reflecting everything that is above it
and I dip the tip of my index finger creating a myriad of ripples

I step back to take it all in
and admire nature's work in this aesthetic landscape
I relay everything back to you, and I watch you as you close your eyes
and give a smile as you absorb every little word
and you open up your beautiful eyes to me
a tear escapes and runs down my cheek
but you can't even see it
however I hope your heart is happy
as I placed this picturesque scene in your mind

# A last choice

always the last one picked
a discarded tissue left alone
a feeling that is common
and something I am quite used to

no one tried to pick up the pieces
As I fell, broken into a million shards
It isn't about feeling the pain of loneliness
rather it would be the pain of everyone leaving

looming over me like a single darkness
giving me a reminder that I am not enough
not enough for anyone to stick in my life for long
a fear that begins to turn into a horrible reality

I would trade my life with someone else's
but would I want to wish this pain upon them?
it is like I am being haunted by a plague
a sickness that slowly just consumes my entire soul

too paranoid to let anyone new walk in
eventually they will realize they can do better
and I'm left once again in the dust
no longer finding it easy to place my trust

maybe I am doing something
maybe I am the problem in every relation
I am the reckoning that everyone dreads
so they all escape before it is too late

no one can come close to me again
I can't handle the hurt any longer
my heart sinks every time someone leaves
why was I not enough for them to stay

## 4 Elements (haiku)

a glistening wrath
ceasing all life to exist
its flames devour us


remains in silence
an awaited calm arrives
those waves wash away


unseen element
that envelops us everywhere
and we breathe it in


here we walk upon
a carpet made up of dirt
I lay on the ground

# Insomnia

it is approximately 4:34 am
i still can't close my eyes
my brain becomes wired to keep me awake
an overdose of adrenaline shoots up to my head


reaching an nocturnal awakening
in which these periods of restlessness
take its place in manifesting into my life
thus beginning a tiring prevalence


my mind is alert. my heart is alarmed.
I hope it remains transient
I can't take anymore sleepless nights
as I watch the sun set, and rise without blinking an eye

a daytime illusionist dreamer
an awakened consciousness as I wake
my eyes burn a hole in my head
then I close my eyes to start counting numbers

an unnatural situation that I'm stuck in
an endless cycle of waking up in the middle of the night
a dark oblivion filled with chaotic nightmares
the very thing that is within my reach but I can't have


anxious of when this will come to an end
challenging thoughts that I am deprived of
an endless whirl of stealthy nights
another repeat of events where my eyes never close

# Growth

life is filled with inconsistencies
but what remains permanent is how I feel about myself
constant roadblocks that stand in my way
but I move past each one with patience
I can't please everyone around me
but what others think simply does not matter anymore
it used to matter when I didn't receive the validation
of people telling me that I am perfect at what I do
focusing on the things that I love
the very parts of life that give me happiness
and I don't need anyone else to tell me they are proud of me
I notice my own growth from the years I have left behind
a shell that I seem to have broken out of
a newfound sense of independence that I reach for
I confidently say that I am proud of who I have become

■

# Pollution

it crawls into your lungs
rendering them useless
rustic air remains contaminated
making it hard for us to breathe


starting with a crushed can
that we just carelessly throw on the ground
but we don't care the impact it holds
someone else will clean it up anyways


another day another mess
black ink reaches out in the ocean
isn't it strange how no one seems to care?
until it is all just disappears


escalating issues on a global level
stuck cleaning up your litter
an endangerment to the ones that live
all due to a careless mistake

you can't even see the blue skies anymore
concealed with a thick ash gray
the consequences keep piling on top
when will it ever end?


the end of our planet seems to draw near
something so beautiful looks so dreary
this a warning to avoid tarnishing what we have now

## Present, not future

I observe as life runs past me
While I remain stagnant in a single place
Always been too worried to be someone new
And now I just think it's too late

Too busy just living for the future
While everyone else imbued living in the moment
I wasted my years away locked away
I didn't think I was ready for the world yet

Always lent a hand to someone in need
Threw my life away to keep everyone happy
I kept myself evaded from the real truth
That I wasn't ready to live for myself yet

Copious amounts of hurdles thrown our way
Which dismotivate us from keeping strong
We get stuck dwelling in our malicious pasts
Forbidding our souls from healing

We allow strangers into our hearts
Just for them to turn away in times of need
But we can't have ourselves weakened
We can't let our mistakes define our future

You eventually learn with age
A simple fact that helps us continue on the path we take
We all want to do well in our lives
After seeing ourselves struggle for so long

It is our turn to live for ourselves
To wake up to a fresh, spirited day
I allow my fractured selves to heal
And turn over to a new page

# Dead ends

It's been a while since we last spoke
I push myself to ask you how you have been
A question pondered but rather left unanswered
I dread the bottomless pit that grows in my stomach
As I recollect on how much my heart has grieved for you

Can such acts, such behaviors ever be deemed forgivable?
I wait for the day that I can make my heart forget you
Because of empty promises that were spun out of thin air
And salty words that burned like a scar on my skin

In that moment a friend turns to an enemy
Filled with instantaneous regrets after having met you
I struggle to let your arm off of me
Because your grip on me is too tight¨
Leaving a red lash on my pale wrist

A waste of time to believe your negligent words
Struggle to figure if you would be different now
Feeling completely useless in front of you
I start preferring the months we didn't speak
And we reach another dead end.

## BLACK EAGLE BOOKS

www.blackeaglebooks.org
info@blackeaglebooks.org

Black Eagle Books, an independent publisher, was founded as a nonprofit organization in April, 2019. It is our mission to connect and engage the Indian diaspora and the world at large with the best of works of world literature published on a collaborative platform, with special emphasis on foregrounding Contemporary Classics and New Writing.

www.ingramcontent.com/pod-product-compliance
Lightning Source LLC
Chambersburg PA
CBHW020548080526
44583CB00013B/1046